MORAL PRINCIPLES IN EDUCATION

AND

MY PEDAGOGIC CREED

MYERS EDUCATION PRESS

Timely Classics in Education

MORAL PRINCIPLES IN EDUCATION

AND

MY PEDAGOGIC CREED

John Dewey

With a Critical Introduction by
PATRICIA H. HINCHEY

Myers
Education
Press

Copyright © 2019 | Myers Education Press, LLC

Published by Myers Education Press, LLC
P.O. Box 424
Gorham, ME 04038

Myers Education Press is an academic publisher specializing in books, e-books and digital content in the field of education. All of our books are subjected to a rigorous peer review process and produced in compliance with the standards of the Council on Library and Information Resources.

LIBRARY OF CONGRESS CATALOGING-IN-PUBLICATION DATA available from Library of Congress.

13-digit ISBN 978-1-9755-0146-4 (paperback)
13-digit ISBN 978-1-9755-0147-1 (library networkable e-edition)
13-digit ISBN 978-1-9755-0148-8 (consumer e-edition)

Printed in the United States of America.

All first editions printed on acid-free paper that meets the American National Standards Institute Z39-48 standard.

Books published by Myers Education Press may be purchased at special quantity discount rates for groups, workshops, training organizations and classroom usage. Please call our customer service department at 1-800-232-0223 for details.

Cover design by Sophie Appel
Interior design and composition by Rachel Reiss

Visit us on the web at **www.myersedpress.com** to browse our complete list of titles.

Contents

Introduction

When it comes to public education in the United States, some issues never fade. Chief among these are what exactly public schools are for and what professional practice in those schools should look like. Since the founding of the country, many great thinkers following in the footsteps of such giants as Thomas Jefferson and Horace Mann have argued that the chief reason to have public schools at all is to ensure an educated public capable of safeguarding democracy. If they are well-trained in good judgement, educated citizens can be relied on to vote out of office any scoundrels or demagogues who might find their way in. Indeed, Mann called public education "our only political safety."*

And yet, despite centuries of eloquent writing insisting that public schools must focus on developing an educated public prepared to exert good judgement in the political realm, dominant contemporary discourse instead maintains that their primary purpose is to prepare children for adult economic life. Schools are urged to prepare students either for specific jobs to be assumed immediately after high school or to prepare them for higher education, promoted primarily as a route to better paying jobs. Of course, many other ideas about school goals have also circulated over the years, including the idea that schools must "fix" students with "problems" often categorized as moral failings, such as

---

* Quoted in *The New Era*, Vol. III, No.10 (October 1873), p. 368.

laziness, drug use and even poor driving. Moving public schools even farther from their role as guardians of democratic life is the recent notion that "public" schools don't have to be run by public entities; they can instead be run by for-profit providers. Given the profit motive of such operators, it's difficult to imagine their schools educating children to become citizens critical of and dedicated to removing politicians who act in the interest of corporate campaign contributors rather than in the interest of general public welfare.

Yet even as such forces tug (or shove) schools this way and that in terms of their goals, there is a critical need for public schools to embrace their historical responsibility to nurture a public that can and will effectively use their voting power to protect American democratic institutions. In contrast to that expectation, in 2018, segments of voters made several convicted criminals viable Congressional candidates. For example, six felons ran for Congress in 2018, including one former sheriff convicted of criminal contempt of court after ignoring a court order to stop illegally detaining people based on race; another was a mine owner convicted not only of tax evasion but also of evading safety laws—after 29 workers died in one of his mines.[*] Since persisting in illegal racial discrimination and risking the lives of workers raise considerable question about how well these candidates might be expected to protect and defend the welfare of the general population, it's reasonable to question the judgement of the voters who supported them. Moreover, in the single month of August that year, one Congressman was arrested for insider trading[†] while another was indicted for wire fraud, falsifying records, campaign finance violations and conspiracy.[‡]

---

[*] Swier, R. (2018, January 18). Six convicted felons are running for the U.S. Congress in 2018. Retrieved from https://drrichswier.com/2018/01/18/six-convicted-felons-are-running-for-the-u-s-congress-in-2018/

[†] Feuer, Al. and Goldmacher, S. (2018, August 8). New York Congressman Chris Collins is charged with insider trading. *New York Times*. Retrieved from https://www.nytimes.com/2018/08/08/nyregion/chris-collins-insider-trading.html

[‡] Jarrett, L. and Reston, M. (2018, August 22). Rep. Duncan Hunter and his wife indicted in use of campaign funds for personal expenses. *CNN*. Retrieved from

Political races and events in prior years offer a wealth of other examples. While it's true that a crime can be minor and a criminal reformed, a Wikipedia list of federal politicians convicted of many serious crimes suggests that the voting public has not generally done an admirable job of critically assessing political candidates or monitoring corruption in government institutions. Since the American voting system is the citizens' tool to ensure honest and effective government, both the public's disappointing screening of candidates and the typically abysmally low voter turnout of 40-60%* are worrisome. In the end, the failure of politicians to represent the interests of their constituents reflects the failure of the voting public to act, and act wisely, in the political realm. In addition, contemporary political discourse is misleading or untruthful and often starkly ugly as well, demonizing anyone who happens to be on the other side of any issue. Meanwhile, severe inequities in wealth and opportunity—the kind that historically have sparked the downfall of countless regimes around the globe—have been steadily emerging in the United States, often aided by federal policy in such areas as taxation and regulation.

In short, government in the United States is not working well for too many of its citizens in the second decade of the twenty-first century. Americans appear to be a generally unhappy population,† and there is some evidence that seeing little improvement in their lives and losing optimism about the future led many voters in the 2016 presidential election to support Donald Trump,‡ perceived as an outsider who might shake up the status quo. Subsequent to that election, the country's deep economic, social and political divisions have shown signs of nudging some segments

---

https://www.cnn.com/2018/08/21/politics/duncan-hunter-campaign-charges/index.html

* Fair Vote. (n.d.) http://www.fairvote.org/voter_turnout#voter_turnout_101

† Shen, L. (2017, March 20). Americans may be rich, but they're not happy. *Fortune*. Retrieved from http://fortune.com/2017/03/20/america-world-happiness-report/

‡ Florida, R. (2018, April 26). How unhappiness helped elect Trump. *Citylab*. Retrieved from https://www.citylab.com/life/2018/04/how-unhappiness-helped-elect-trump/558950/

of the population steadily closer to violence.* Given contemporary conditions, it is imperative to reconsider and reanimate calls for schools to educate a public more effective in holding politicians to account for the welfare of the general population through peaceful, democratic processes.

The relevance of Dewey's work to pressing contemporary issues is clearly stated in the unattributed Introduction to the original edition of *Moral Principles in Education*. In it, readers are cautioned about the future when those in charge of schools

> would not have the children learn to govern themselves and one another, but would have the masters rule them, ignoring the fact that this common practice in childhood may be a foundation for that evil condition in adult society where the citizens are arbitrarily ruled by political bosses.

Current abuses of political power suggest American society has now largely entered just such an "evil condition." However, as the Introduction states, we can turn to Dewey to find direction as we consider how to reorient public schools to their original democratic purpose—to educate a public that can and will effectively protect the democratic society.

As a seminal text, *Democracy and Education*, of course, explicitly details how and why he sees the two areas as inextricably linked. In *Moral Principles in Education,* Dewey reiterates his essential rationale. Because all humans are immersed in specific societies, both individuals and the institutions they create are inescapably influenced by their societies. The role of education, whether in apprenticeships or brick-and-mortar classrooms, is to prepare the young to sustain and improve their society by executing their adult roles well, acting in prosocial ways because of habits and values internalized earlier. Education is, he asserts, "the fundamental method of social progress and reform."

---

* Zanona, M. (2017, August 27). Threats of political violence rise in polarized Trump era. *The Hill*. Retrieved from http://thehill.com/homenews/administration/348014-threats-of-political-violence-rise-in-polarized-trump-era

In formal education systems, such values and habits cannot be learned if schools are divorced from society—that is, if actions, social or otherwise, are divorced from context. Dewey illustrates with this anecdote:

> [T]here is a swimming school in a certain city where youth are taught to swim without going into the water, being repeatedly drilled in the various movements which are necessary for swimming. When one of the young men so trained was asked what he did when he got into the water, he laconically replied, "Sunk."

The story, he asserts, is true.

Dewey argues that in contrast to such inauthentic sterile environments, every school and class must be a genuine society where the behaviors wanted tomorrow are practiced in meaningful context today: "There cannot be two sets of ethical principles, one for life in the school, and the other for life outside of the school." If we want not only the electorate but also political, corporate and other leaders to act in ways that support rather than weaken democratic society, then life in schools must model the life we hope for outside them: "We cannot smother and repress the child's powers, or gradually abort them (from failure of opportunity for exercise), and then expect a character with initiative and consecutive industry." School life must provide real opportunities for children to contribute as well as receive, to teach as well as to learn, and to lead as well as to follow. Dewey argues that individuals who experience such education will enter their adult roles having already adopted prosocial and effective habits of thinking and acting, and that society at large—including government and other institutions—will simultaneously improve.

In both works presented in this text, *Moral Principles in Education* and *Pedagogic Creed*, Dewey also has much to say about ubiquitous ideas and practices in schools that conflict with or undermine his vision. These ideas include that:

- the point of education is not for life today but for life at some distant point in time (next year's math class, or admission to college, or a line on a resumé);
- talking at students will change their behavior; giving them information will result in their good judgement;
- a curriculum of discrete subjects, each learned for its own sake without connection to students' lives, is appropriate or desirable;
- student interest is irrelevant to determining academic content;
- all students should do the same work at the same time; and
- threats and punishments effectively shape long term behavior.

Unfortunately, though Dewey identified these ideas as counterproductive over a century ago, they remain widely entrenched in public schools today. Not surprisingly, in fact, many educators are understandably as dispirited about the current state of American education as much of the general public appears to be about the current state of American politics and government.

As many political writers are urging, however, now is hardly the time to give up—either on the truly democratic society Americans have been working toward for over two hundred years now, or on the public schools that likely constitute the best hope for its future. Many educators today, like many before them, persist in working toward the kinds of schools Dewey imagined. Just a small sampling of current indicators makes clear that a growing number of professionals continue to promote the goals Dewey espoused. Since 1936, for example, The John Dewey Society has continued "to keep alive John Dewey's commitment to the use of critical and reflective intelligence in the search for solutions to crucial problems in education and culture."[*] The organization continues facilitating communication among like-minded educators. It also supports their efforts toward school reform in multiple ways, including a Democracy in Education initiative intended to explore ways to "reclaim our schools and higher education institutions as civic anchors of

---

[*] http://www.johndeweysociety.org

our democracy."* Many of Dewey's principles are also embedded in a 2013 position paper from the National Council for Social Studies titled "Revitalizing Civic Learning in Our Schools," which cites Dewey in its call for schools to educate citizens who are

> concerned for the rights and welfare of others, socially responsible, willing to listen to alternative perspectives, confident in their capacity to make a difference, and ready to contribute personally to civic and political action. They strike a reasonable balance between their own interests and the common good.†

Yet another contributor to reform efforts is the Rethinking Schools organization, which is "firmly committed to equity and to the vision that public education is central to the creation of a humane, caring, multiracial democracy."‡ Rethinking Schools publishes educational materials widely used both nationally and internationally in opposition to anti-democratic school practices and curriculum.

Yet, despite the many efforts of such organizations and countless individual educators, the vision of public schools both as a critical tool for social improvement and as the safeguard of democracy remains aspirational—as it always has been. As the Rethinking Schools website points out, "That this vision has yet to be fully realized does not mean it should be abandoned." Dewey's vision is a grand one that educators cannot expect to fully realize in any single lifetime, given the constant struggle for control of American hearts and minds. After all, the for-profit corporations controlling many charter schools and profiting from online education today are simply the current manifestation of the business interests that led to Harold Rugg's progressive social studies

---

* http://www.johndeweysociety.org/democracy-in-education-initiative/sign-collective-die-founding-statement/

† https://www.socialstudies.org/positions/revitalizing_civic_learning

‡ *Rethinking Schools.* (2017). History. Retrieved from https://www.rethinking-schools.org/pages/history

textbooks being banned and burned 1939-1941—as undemocratic an action as can be imagined.

Sadly, we have to acknowledge that repeated threats to any democratic society are to be expected, since greed for wealth and power emerge regularly in societies the world over. If this were not the case, the nation's founders would not have established multiple defenses against efforts to return power to a handful of leaders. Educators are on the front lines of those defenses. By following in Dewey's footsteps, they live out their historic responsibility and do much to undo the damage now being done to American democratic life every day.

MORAL PRINCIPLES IN EDUCATION

Introduction[*]

Education as a public business

It is one of the complaints of the schoolmaster that the public does not defer to his professional opinion as completely as it does to that of practitioners in other professions. At first sight it might seem as though this indicated a defect either in the public or in the profession; and yet a wider view of the situation would suggest that such a conclusion is not a necessary one. The relations of education to the public are different from those of any other professional work. Education is a public business with us, in a sense that the protection and restoration of personal health or legal rights are not. To an extent characteristic of no other institution, save that of the state itself, the school has power to modify the social order. And under our political system, it is the right

---

[*] The wording of the last paragraph of this introduction (p. 6) suggests that someone other than Dewey wrote the piece. It seems likely (though not certain) that the editor of the original Houghton Mifflin edition, Henry Suzzallo, is the author of these introductory remarks.

3

of each individual to have a voice in the making of social policies as, indeed, he has a vote in the determination of political affairs. If this be true, education is primarily a public business, and only secondarily a specialized vocation. The layman, then, will always have his right to some utterance on the operation of the public schools.

Education as expert service

I have said "some utterance," but not "all"; for school-mastering has its own special mysteries, its own knowledge and skill into which the untrained layman cannot penetrate. We are just beginning to recognize that the school and the government have a common problem in this respect. Education and politics are two functions fundamentally controlled by public opinion. Yet the conspicuous lack of efficiency and economy in the school and in the state has quickened our recognition of a larger need for expert service. But just where shall public opinion justly express itself, and what shall properly be left to expert judgment?

The relations of expert opinion and public opinion

In so far as broad policies and ultimate ends affecting the welfare of all are to be determined, the public may well claim its right to settle issues by the vote or voice of majorities. But the selection and prosecution of the detailed ways and means by which the public will is to be executed efficiently must remain largely a matter of specialized and expert service. To the superior knowledge and technique required here, the public may well defer.

In the conduct of the schools, it is well for the citizens to determine the ends proper to them, and it is their privilege to judge of the efficacy of results. Upon questions that concern all the manifold details by which children are to be converted into desirable types of men and women, the expert schoolmaster should be authoritative, at least to a degree commensurate with his superior knowledge of this very complex problem. The administration of the schools, the making of the course of study, the selection of texts, the prescription of methods of teaching, these are matters with which the people, or their representatives upon boards of education, cannot deal save with danger of becoming mere meddlers.

The discussion of moral education an illustration of mistaken views of laymen

Nowhere is the validity of this distinction between education as a public business and education as an expert professional service brought out more clearly than in an analysis of the public discussion of the moral work of the school. How frequently of late have those unacquainted with the special nature of the school proclaimed the moral ends of education and at the same time demanded direct ethical instruction as the particular method by which they were to be realized! This, too, in spite of the fact that those who know best the powers and limitations of instruction as an instrument have repeatedly pointed out the futility of assuming that knowledge of right constitutes a guarantee of right doing. How common it is for those who assert that education is for social efficiency to assume that the school should return to the barren discipline of the traditional formal subjects, reading, writing, and the rest! This, too, regardless of the fact that it has taken a century of educational evolution to make the course of study varied and rich enough to call for those impulses and activities of social life which need training in the child. And how many who speak glowingly of the large services of the public schools to a democracy of free and self-reliant men affect a cynical and even vehement opposition to the "self-government of schools"! These would not have the children learn to govern themselves and one another, but would have the masters rule them, ignoring the fact that this common practice in childhood may be a foundation for that evil condition in adult society where the citizens are arbitrarily ruled by political bosses.

One need not cite further cases of the incompetence of the lay public to deal with technical questions of school methods. Instances are plentiful to show that well-meaning people, competent enough to judge of the aims and results of school work, make a mistake in insisting upon the prerogative of directing the technical aspects of education with a dogmatism that would not characterize their statements regarding any other special field of knowledge or action.

A *fundamental understanding of moral principles in education*

Nothing can be more useful than for the public and the teaching profession to understand their respective functions. The teacher needs to understand public opinion and the social order, as much as the public needs to comprehend the nature of expert educational service. It will take time to draw the boundary lines that will be conducive to respect, restraint, and efficiency in those concerned; but a beginning can be made upon fundamental matters, and nothing so touches the foundations of our educational thought as a discussion of the moral principles in education.

It is our pleasure to present a treatment of them by a thinker whose vital influence upon the reform of school methods is greater than that of any of his contemporaries. In his discussion of the social and psychological factors in moral education, there is much that will suggest what social opinion should determine, and much that will indicate what must be left to the trained teacher and school official.

The Moral Purpose
of the School

An English contemporary philosopher has called attention to the difference between moral ideas and ideas about morality. "Moral ideas" are ideas of any sort whatsoever which take effect in conduct and improve it, make it better than it otherwise would be. Similarly, one may say, immoral ideas are ideas of whatever sort (whether arithmetical or geographical or physiological) which show themselves in making behavior worse than it would otherwise be; and non-moral ideas, one may say, are such ideas and pieces of information as leave conduct uninfluenced for either the better or the worse. Now "ideas about morality" may be morally indifferent or immoral or moral. There is nothing in the nature of ideas *about* morality, of information *about* honesty or purity or kindness which automatically transmutes such ideas into good character or good conduct.

This distinction between moral ideas, ideas of any sort whatsoever that have become a part of character and hence a part of the working motives of behavior, and ideas *about* moral action that may remain as inert and ineffective as if they were so much knowledge about Egyptian archæology, is fundamental to the discussion of moral education.

The business of the educator—whether parent or teacher—is to see to it that the greatest possible number of ideas acquired by children and youth are acquired in such a vital way that they become *moving* ideas, motive-forces in the guidance of conduct. This demand and this opportunity make the moral purpose universal and dominant in all instruction—whatsoever the topic. Were it not for this possibility, the familiar statement that the ultimate purpose of all education is character-forming would be hypocritical pretense; for as every one knows, the direct and immediate attention of teachers and pupils must be, for the greater part of the time, upon intellectual matters. It is out of the question to keep direct moral considerations constantly uppermost.

> *The business of the educator—whether parent or teacher—is to see to it that the greatest possible number of ideas acquired by children and youth are acquired in such a vital way that they become* moving *ideas, motive-forces in the guidance of conduct.*

But it is not out of the question to aim at making the methods of learning, of acquiring intellectual power, and of assimilating subject-matter, such that they will render behavior more enlightened, more consistent, more vigorous than it otherwise would be.

The same distinction between "moral ideas" and "ideas about morality" explains for us a source of continual misunderstanding between teachers in the schools and critics of education outside of the schools. The latter look through the school programmes, the school courses of study, and do not find any place set apart for instruction in ethics or for "moral teaching." Then they assert that the schools are doing nothing, or next to nothing, for character-training; they become emphatic, even vehement, about the moral deficiencies of public education. The schoolteachers, on the other hand, resent these criticisms as an injustice, and hold not only that they do "teach morals," but that they teach them every moment of the day, five days in the week. In this contention the teachers *in principle* are in the right; if they are in the wrong, it is not because special periods are not set aside for what after all can only be teaching *about* morals, but because their own characters, or their school atmosphere and ideals, or their methods of teaching, or the subject-matter which they teach, are not such *in detail* as to bring intellectual results into vital union with character so that they become working forces in behavior. Without discussing, therefore, the limits or the value of so-called direct moral instruction (or, better, instruction *about* morals), it may be laid down as fundamental that the influence of direct moral instruction, even at its very best, is *comparatively* small in amount and slight in influence, when the whole field of moral growth through education is taken into account. This larger field of indirect and vital moral education, the development of character through all the agencies, instrumentalities, and materials of school life is, therefore, the subject of our present discussion.

The Moral Training Given by the School Community

There cannot be two sets of ethical principles, one for life in the school, and the other for life outside of the school. As conduct is one, so also the principles of conduct are one. The tendency to discuss the morals of the school as if the school were an institution by itself is highly unfortunate. The moral responsibility of the school, and of those who conduct it, is to society. The school is fundamentally an institution erected by society to do a certain specific work,—to exercise a certain specific function in maintaining the life and advancing the welfare of society. The educational system which does not recognize that this fact entails upon it an ethical responsibility is derelict and a defaulter. It is not doing what it was called into existence to do, and what it pretends to do. Hence the entire structure of the school in general and its concrete workings in particular need to be considered from time to time with reference to the social position and function of the school.

There cannot be two sets of ethical principles, one for life in the school, and the other for life outside of the school.

The idea that the moral work and worth of the public school system as a whole are to be measured by its social value is, indeed, a familiar notion. However, it is frequently taken in too limited and rigid a way. The social work of the school is often limited to training for citizenship, and citizenship is then interpreted in a narrow sense as meaning capacity to vote intelligently, disposition to obey laws, etc. But it is futile to contract and cramp the ethical responsibility of the school in this way. The child is one, and he must either live his social life as an integral unified being, or suffer loss and create friction. To pick out one of the many social relations which the child bears, and to define the work of the school by that alone, is like instituting a vast and complicated system of physical exercise which would have for its object simply the development of the lungs and the power of breathing, independent of other organs and functions. The child is an organic whole, intellectually, socially, and morally, as well as physically. We must take the child as a member of society in the broadest sense, and demand for and from the schools whatever is necessary to enable the child intelligently to recognize all his social relations and take his part in sustaining them.

To isolate the formal relationship of citizenship from the whole system of relations with which it is actually interwoven; to suppose that there is some one particular study or mode of treatment which can make the child a good citizen; to suppose, in other words, that a good citizen is anything more than a thoroughly efficient and serviceable member of society, one with all his powers of body and mind under control, is a hampering superstition which it is hoped may soon disappear from educational discussion.

The child is to be not only a voter and a subject of law; he is also to be a member of a family, himself in turn responsible, in all probability, for rearing and training of future children, thereby maintaining the continuity of society. He is to be a worker, engaged in some occupation which will be of use to society, and which will maintain his own independence and self-respect. He is to be a member of some particular neighborhood and community, and must contribute to the values of life, add to the decencies and graces of civilization wherever he is. These are bare and formal statements, but if we let our imagination translate them into their concrete details, we have a wide and varied scene. For the child properly to take his place in reference to these various functions means training in science, in art, in history; means command of the fundamental methods of inquiry and the fundamental tools of intercourse and communication; means a trained and sound body, skillful eye and hand; means habits of industry, perseverance; in short, habits of serviceableness.

Moreover, the society of which the child is to be a member is, in the United States, a democratic and progressive society. The child must be educated for leadership as well as for obedience. He must have power of self-direction and power of directing others, power of administration, ability to assume positions of responsibility. This necessity of educating for leadership is as great on the industrial as on the political side.

> *The child must be educated for leadership as well as for obedience.*

New inventions, new machines, new methods of transportation and intercourse are making over the whole scene of action year by year. It is an absolute impossibility to educate the child for any fixed station in life. So far as education is conducted unconsciously or consciously on this basis, it results in fitting the future citizen for no station in life, but makes him a drone, a hanger-on, or an actual retarding influence in the onward movement. Instead of caring for himself and for others, he becomes one who has himself to be cared for. Here, too, the ethical responsibility of the school on the social side must be interpreted in the broadest and freest spirit; it is equivalent to that training of the child which will give him such possession of himself that he may take charge of himself; may not only adapt himself to the changes that are going on, but have power to shape and direct them.

Apart from participation in social life, the school has no moral end nor aim. As long as we confine ourselves to the school as an isolated institution, we have no directing principles, because we have no object. For example, the end of education is said to be the harmonious development of all the powers of the individual. Here no reference to social life or membership is apparent, and yet many think we have in it an adequate and thoroughgoing definition of the goal of education. But if this definition be taken independently of social relationship we have no way of telling what is meant by any one of the terms employed. We do not know what a power is; we do not know what development is; we do not know what harmony is. A power is a power only with ref-

Apart from participation in social life, the school has no moral end nor aim.

erence to the use to which it is put, the function it has to serve. If we leave out the uses supplied by social life we have nothing but the old "faculty psychology" to tell what is meant by power and what the specific powers are. The principle reduces itself to enumerating a lot of faculties like perception, memory, reasoning, etc., and then stating that each one of these powers needs to be developed.

Education then becomes a gymnastic exercise. Acute powers of observation and memory might be developed by studying Chinese characters; acuteness in reasoning might be got by discussing the scholastic subtleties of the Middle Ages. The simple fact is that there is no isolated faculty of observation, or memory, or reasoning any more than there is an original faculty of blacksmithing, carpentering, or steam engineering. Faculties mean simply that particular impulses and habits have been coördinated or framed with reference to accomplishing certain definite kinds of work. We need to know the social situations in which the individual will have to use ability to observe, recollect, imagine, and reason, in order to have any way of telling what a training of mental powers actually means.

What holds in the illustration of this particular definition of education holds good from whatever point of view we approach the matter. Only as we interpret school activities with reference to the larger circle of social activities to which they relate do we find any standard for judging their moral significance.

The school itself must be a vital social institution to a much greater extent than obtains at present. I am told that there is a swimming school in a certain city where youth are taught to swim without going into the water, being repeatedly drilled in the various movements which are necessary for swimming. When one of the young men so trained was asked what he did when he got into the water, he laconically replied, "Sunk." The story happens to be true; were it not, it would seem to be a fable made expressly for the purpose of typifying the ethical relationship of school to society. The school cannot be a preparation for social life excepting as it reproduces, within itself, typical conditions of social life. At present it is largely engaged in the futile task of Sisyphus. It is endeavoring to form habits in children for use in a social life which, it would almost seem, is carefully and purposely kept away from vital contact with the child undergoing training. The only way to prepare for social life is to engage in social life. To form habits of social usefulness and serviceableness apart from any direct social need and motive, apart from any existing social situation, is, to the letter, teaching the child to swim by going through motions outside of the water. The most indispensable condition is left out of account, and the results are correspondingly partial.

The much lamented separation in the schools of intellectual and moral training, of acquiring information and growing in character, is simply one expression of the failure to conceive and construct the school as a social institution, having social life and value within itself. Except so far as the school is an embryonic typical community life, moral training must be partly pathological and partly formal. Training is pathological when stress is laid upon correcting wrong-doing instead of upon forming habits of positive service. Too often the teacher's concern with the moral life of pupils takes the form of alertness for failures to conform to school rules and routine. These regulations, judged from the standpoint of the development of the child at the time, are more or less conventional and arbitrary. They are rules which have to be made in order that the existing modes of school work may go on; but the lack of inherent necessity in these school modes reflects itself in a feeling, on the part of the child, that the moral discipline of the school is arbitrary. Any conditions that compel the teacher to take note of failures rather than of healthy growth give false standards and result in distortion and perversion. Attending to wrong-doing ought to be an incident rather than a principle. The child ought to have a positive consciousness of what he is about, so as to judge his acts from the standpoint of reference to the work which he has to do. Only in this way does he have a vital standard, one that enables him to turn failures to account for the future.

By saying that the moral training of the school is formal, I mean that the moral habits currently emphasized by the school are habits which are created, as it were, *ad hoc*. Even the habits of promptness, regularity, industry, non-interference with the work of others, faithfulness to tasks imposed, which are specially inculcated in the school, are habits that are necessary simply because the school system is what it is, and must be preserved intact. If we grant the inviolability of the school system as it is, these habits represent permanent and necessary moral ideas; but just in so far as the school system is itself isolated and mechanical, insistence upon these moral habits is more or less unreal, because the ideal to which they relate is not itself necessary. The duties, in other words, are distinctly school duties, not life duties. If we compare this condition with that of the well-ordered home, we find that the duties and responsibilities that the child has there to recognize do not belong to the family as a specialized and isolated institution, but flow from the very nature of the social life in which the family participates and to which it contributes. The child ought to have the same motives for right doing and to be judged by the same standards in the school, as the adult in the wider social life to which he belongs. Interest in community welfare, an interest that is intellectual and practical, as well as emotional—an interest, that is to say, in perceiving whatever makes for social order and progress, and in carrying these principles into execution—is the moral habit to which all the special school habits must be related if they are to be animated by the breath of life.

The Moral Training from Methods of Instruction

The principle of the social character of the school as the basic factor in the moral education given may be also applied to the question of methods of instruction,—not in their details, but their general spirit. The emphasis then falls upon construction and giving out, rather than upon absorption and mere learning. We fail to recognize how essentially individualistic the latter methods are, and how unconsciously, yet certainly and effectively, they react into the child's ways of judging and of acting. Imagine forty children all engaged in reading the same books, and in preparing and reciting the same lessons day after day. Suppose this process constitutes by far the larger part of their work, and that they are continually judged from the standpoint of what they are able to take in in a study hour and reproduce in a recitation hour. There is next to no opportunity for any social division of labor. There is no opportunity for each child to work out something specifically his own, which he may contribute to the common stock, while he, in turn, participates in the productions of others. All are set to do exactly the same work and turn out the same products. The social spirit is not cultivated,—in fact, in so far as the purely individualistic method gets in its work, it atrophies for lack of use. One reason why reading aloud in school is poor is that the real motive for the use of language—the desire to communicate and to learn—is not utilized. The child knows perfectly well that the teacher and all his fellow pupils have exactly the same facts and ideas before them that he has; he is not *giving* them anything at all. And it may be questioned whether the moral lack is not as great as the intellectual. The child is born with a natural desire to give out, to do, to serve. When this tendency is not used, when conditions are such that other motives are substituted, the accumulation of an influence working against the social spirit is much larger than we have any idea of,—especially when the burden of work, week after week, and year after year, falls upon this side.

But lack of cultivation of the social spirit is not all. Positively individualistic motives and standards are inculcated. Some stimulus must be found to keep the child at his studies. At the best this will be his affection for his teacher, together with a feeling that he is not violating school rules, and thus negatively, if not positively, is contributing to the good of the school. I have nothing to say against these motives so far as they go, but they are inadequate. The relation between the piece of work to be done and affection for a third person is external, not intrinsic. It is therefore liable to break down whenever the external conditions are changed. Moreover, this attachment to a particular person, while in a way social, may become so isolated and exclusive as to be selfish in quality. In any case, the child should gradually grow out of this relatively external motive into an appreciation, for its own sake, of the social value of what he has to do, because of its larger relations to life, not pinned down to two or three persons.

But, unfortunately, the motive is not always at this relative best, but mixed with lower motives which are distinctly egoistic. Fear is a motive which is almost sure to enter in,—not necessarily physical fear, or fear of punishment, but fear of losing the approbation of others; or fear of failure, so extreme as to be morbid and paralyzing. On the other side, emulation and rivalry enter in. Just because all are doing the same work, and are judged (either in recitation or examination with reference to grading and to promotion) not from the standpoint of their personal contribution, but from that of *comparative* success, the feeling of superiority over others is unduly appealed to, while timid children are depressed. Children are judged with reference to their capacity to realize the same external standard. The weaker gradually lose their sense of power, and accept a position of continuous and persistent inferiority. The effect upon both self-respect and respect for work need not be dwelt upon. The strong learn to glory, not in their strength, but in the fact that they are stronger. The child is prematurely launched into the region of individualistic competition, and this in a direction where competition is least applicable, namely, in intellectual and artistic matters, whose law is coöperation and participation.

Next, perhaps, to the evils of passive absorption and of competition for external standing come, perhaps, those which result from the eternal emphasis upon preparation for a remote future. I do not refer here to the waste of energy and vitality that accrues when children, who live so largely in the immediate present, are appealed to in the name of a dim and uncertain future which means little or nothing to them. I have in mind rather the habitual procrastination that develops when the motive for work is future, not present; and the false standards of judgment that are created when work is estimated, not on the basis of present need and present responsibility, but by reference to an external result, like passing an examination, getting promoted, entering high school, getting into college, etc. Who can reckon up the loss of moral power that arises from the constant impression that nothing is worth doing in itself, but only as a preparation for something else, which in turn is only a getting ready for some genuinely serious end beyond? Moreover, as a rule, it will be found that remote success is an end which appeals most to those in whom egoistic desire to get ahead—to get ahead of others—is already only too strong a motive. Those in whom personal ambition is already so strong that it paints glowing pictures of future victories may be touched; others of a more generous nature do not respond.

I cannot stop to paint the other side. I can only say that the introduction of every method that appeals to the child's active powers, to his capacities in construction, production, and creation, marks an opportunity to shift the centre of ethical gravity from an absorption which is selfish to a service which is social. Manual training is more than manual; it is more than intellectual; in the hands of any good teacher it lends itself easily, and almost as a matter of course, to development of social habits. Ever since the philosophy of Kant, it has been a commonplace of æsthetic theory, that art is universal; that it is not the product of purely personal desire or appetite, or capable of merely individual appropriation, but has a value participated in by all who perceive it. Even in the schools where most conscious attention is paid to moral considerations, the methods of study and recitation may be such as to emphasize appreciation rather than power, an emotional readiness to assimilate the experiences of others, rather than enlightened and trained capacity to carry forward those values which in other conditions and past times made those experiences worth having. At all events, separation between instruction and character continues in our schools (in spite of the efforts of individual teachers) as a result of divorce between learning and doing. The attempt to attach genuine moral effectiveness to the mere processes of learning, and to the habits which go along with learning, can result only in a training infected with formality, arbitrariness, and an undue emphasis upon failure to conform. That there is as much accomplished as there is shows the possibilities involved in methods of school activity which afford opportunity for reciprocity, coöperation, and positive personal achievement.

The Social Nature of the Course of Study

In many respects, it is the subject-matter used in school life which decides both the general atmosphere of the school and the methods of instruction and discipline which rule. A barren "course of study," that is to say, a meagre and narrow field of school activities, cannot possibly lend itself to the development of a vital social spirit or to methods that appeal to sympathy and coöperation instead of to absorption, exclusiveness, and competition. Hence it becomes an all important matter to know how we shall apply our social standard of moral value to the subject-matter of school work, to what we call, traditionally, the "studies" that occupy pupils.

A study is to be considered as a means of bringing the child to realize the social scene of action. Thus considered it gives a criterion for selection of material and for judgment of values. We have at present three independent values set up: one of culture, another of information, and another of discipline. In reality, these refer only to three phases of social interpretation. Information is genuine or educative only in so far as it presents definite images and conceptions of materials placed in a context of social life. Discipline is genuinely educative only as it represents a reaction of information into the individual's own powers so that he brings them under control for social ends. Culture, if it is to be genuinely educative and not an external polish or factitious varnish, represents the vital union of information and discipline. It marks the socialization of the individual in his outlook upon life.

This point may be illustrated by brief reference to a few of the school studies. In the first place, there is no line of demarkation within facts themselves which classifies them as belonging to science, history, or geography, respectively. The pigeon-hole classification which is so prevalent at present (fostered by introducing the pupil at the outset into a number of different studies contained in different text-books) gives an utterly erroneous idea of the relations of studies to one another and to the intellectual whole to which all belong. In fact, these subjects have to do with the same ultimate reality, namely, the conscious experience of man. It is only because we have different interests, or different ends, that we sort out the material and label part of it science, part of it history, part geography, and so on. Each "sorting" represents materials arranged with reference to some one dominant typical aim or process of the social life.

This social criterion is necessary, not only to mark off studies from one another, but also to grasp the reasons for each study,—the motives in connection with which it shall be presented. How, for example, should we define geography? What is the unity in the different so-called divisions of geography,—mathematical geography, physical geography, political geography, commercial geography? Are they purely empirical classifications dependent upon the brute fact that we run across a lot of different facts? Or is there some intrinsic principle through which the material is distributed under these various heads,—something in the interest and attitude of the human mind towards them? I should say that geography has to do with all those aspects of social life which are concerned with the interaction of the life of man and nature; or, that it has to do with the world considered as the scene of social interaction. Any fact, then, will be geographical in so far as it has to do with the dependence of man upon his natural environment, or with changes introduced in this environment through the life of man.

The four forms of geography referred to above represent, then, four increasing stages of abstraction in discussing the mutual relation of human life and nature. The beginning must be social geography, the frank recognition of the earth as the home of men acting in relations to one another. I mean by this that the essence of any geographical fact is the consciousness of two persons, or two groups of persons, who are at once separated and connected by their physical environment, and that the interest is in seeing how these people are at once kept apart and brought together in their actions by the instrumentality of the physical environment. The ultimate significance of lake, river, mountain, and plain is not physical but social; it is the part which it plays in modifying and directing human relationships. This evidently involves an extension of the term commercial. It has to do not simply with business, in the narrow sense, but with whatever relates to human intercourse and intercommunication as affected by natural forms and properties. Political geography represents this same social interaction taken in a static instead of in a dynamic way; taken, that is, as temporarily crystallized and fixed in certain forms. Physical geography (including under this not simply physiography, but also the study of flora and fauna) represents a further analysis or abstraction. It studies the conditions which determine human action, leaving out of account, temporarily, the ways in which they concretely do this. Mathematical geography carries the analysis back to more ultimate and remote conditions, showing that the physical conditions of the earth are not ultimate, but depend upon the place which the world occupies in a larger system. Here, in other words, are traced, step by step, the links which connect the immediate social occupations and groupings of men with the whole natural system which ultimately conditions them. Step by step the scene is enlarged and the image of what enters into the make-up of social action is widened and broadened; at no time is the chain of connection to be broken.

It is out of the question to take up the studies one by one and show that their meaning is similarly controlled by social considerations. But I cannot forbear saying a word or two upon history. History is vital or dead to the child according as it is, or is not, presented from the sociological standpoint. When treated simply as a record of what has passed and gone, it must be mechanical, because the past, as the past, is remote. Simply as the past there is no motive for attending to it. The ethical value of history teaching will be measured by the extent to which past events are made the means of understanding the present,—affording insight into what makes up the structure and working of society to-day. Existing social structure is exceedingly complex. It is practically impossible for the child to attack it *en masse* and get any definite mental image of it. But type phases of historical development may be selected which will exhibit, as through a telescope, the essential constituents of the existing order. Greece, for example, represents what art and growing power of individual expression stand for; Rome exhibits the elements and forces of political life on a tremendous scale. Or, as these civilizations are themselves relatively complex, a study of still simpler forms of hunting, nomadic, and agricultural life in the beginnings of civilization, a study of the effects of the introduction of iron, and iron tools, reduces the complexity to simpler elements.

One reason historical teaching is usually not more effective is that the student is set to acquire information in such a way that no epochs or factors stand out in his mind as typical; everything is reduced to the same dead level. The way to secure the necessary perspective is to treat the past as if it were a projected present with some of its elements enlarged.

The principle of contrast is as important as that of similarity. Because the present life is so close to us, touching us at every point, we cannot get away from it to see it as it really is. Nothing stands out clearly or sharply as characteristic. In the study of past periods, attention necessarily attaches itself to striking differences. Thus the child gets a locus of imagination, through which he can remove himself from the pressure of present surrounding circumstances and define them.

History is equally available in teaching the *methods* of social progress. It is commonly stated that history must be studied from the standpoint of cause and effect. The truth of this statement depends upon its interpretation. Social life is so complex and the various parts of it are so organically related to one another and to the natural environment, that it is impossible to say that this or that thing is the cause of some other particular thing. But the study of history can reveal the main instruments in the discoveries, inventions, new modes of life, etc., which have initiated the great epochs of social advance; and it can present to the child types of the main lines of social progress, and can set before him what have been the chief difficulties and obstructions in the way of progress. Once more this can be done only in so far as it is recognized that social forces in themselves are always the same,—that the same kind of influences were at work one hundred and one thousand years ago that are now working,—and that particular historical epochs afford illustration of the way in which the fundamental forces work.

Everything depends, then, upon history being treated from a social standpoint; as manifesting the agencies which have influenced social development and as presenting the typical institutions in which social life has expressed itself. The culture-epoch theory, while working in the right direction, has failed to recognize the importance of treating past periods with relation to the present,—as affording insight into the representative factors of its structure; it has treated these periods too much as if they had some meaning or value in themselves. The way in which the biographical method is handled illustrates the same point. It is often treated in such a way as to exclude from the child's consciousness (or at least not sufficiently to emphasize) the social forces and principles involved in the association of the masses of men. It is quite true that the child is easily interested in history from the biographical standpoint; but unless "the hero" is treated in relation to the community life behind him that he sums up and directs, there is danger that history will reduce itself to a mere exciting story. Then moral instruction reduces itself to drawing certain lessons from the life of the particular personalities concerned, instead of widening and deepening the child's imagination of social relations, ideals, and means.

It will be remembered that I am not making these points for their own sake, but with reference to the general principle that when a study is taught as a mode of understanding social life it has positive ethical import. What the normal child continuously needs is not so much isolated moral lessons upon the importance of truthfulness and honesty, or the beneficent results that follow from a particular act of patriotism, as the formation of habits of social imagination and conception.

I take one more illustration, namely, mathematics. This does, or does not, accomplish its full purpose according as it is, or is not, presented as a social tool. The prevailing divorce between information and character, between knowledge and social action, stalks upon the scene here. The moment mathematical study is severed from the place which it occupies with reference to use in social life, it becomes unduly abstract, even upon the purely intellectual side. It is presented as a matter of technical relations and formulæ apart from any end or use. What the study of number suffers from in elementary education is lack of motivation. Back of this and that and the other particular bad method is the radical mistake of treating number as if it were an end in itself, instead of the means of accomplishing some end. Let the child get a consciousness of what is the use of number, of what it really is for, and half the battle is won. Now this consciousness of the use of reason implies some end which is implicitly social.

One of the absurd things in the more advanced study of arithmetic is the extent to which the child is introduced to numerical operations which have no distinctive mathematical principles characterizing them, but which represent certain general principles found in business relationships. To train the child in these operations, while paying no attention to the business realities in which they are of use, or to the conditions of social life which make these business activities necessary, is neither arithmetic nor common sense. The child is called upon to do examples in interest, partnership, banking, brokerage, and so on through a long string, and no pains are taken to see that, in connection with the arithmetic, he has any sense of the social realities involved. This part of arithmetic is essentially sociological in its nature. It ought either to be omitted entirely, or else be taught in connection with a study of the relevant social realities. As we now manage the study, it is the old case of learning to swim apart from the water over again, with correspondingly bad results on the practical side.

In concluding this portion of the discussion, we may say that our conceptions of moral education have been too narrow, too formal, and too pathological. We have associated the term ethical with certain special acts which are labeled virtues and are set off from the mass of other acts, and are still more divorced from the habitual images and motives of the children performing them. Moral instruction is thus associated with teaching about these particular virtues, or with instilling certain sentiments in regard to them. The moral has been conceived in too goody-goody a way. Ultimate moral motives and forces are nothing more or less than social intelligence—the power of observing and comprehending social situations,—and social power—trained capacities of control—at work in the service of social interest and aims. There is no fact which throws light upon the constitution of society, there is no power whose training adds to social resourcefulness that is not moral.

I sum up, then, this part of the discussion by asking your attention to the moral trinity of the school. The demand is for social intelligence, social power, and social interests. Our resources are (1) the life of the school as a social institution in itself; (2) methods of learning and of doing work; and (3) the school studies or curriculum. In so far as the school represents, in its own spirit, a genuine community life; in so far as what are called school discipline, government, order, etc., are the expressions of this inherent social spirit; in so far as the methods used are those that appeal to the active and constructive powers, permitting the child to give out and thus to serve; in so far as the curriculum is so selected and organized as to provide the material for affording the child a consciousness of the world in which he has to play a part, and the demands he has to meet; so far as these ends are met, the school is organized on an ethical basis. So far as general principles are concerned, all the basic ethical requirements are met. The rest remains between the individual teacher and the individual child.

The Psychological Aspect of Moral Education

So far we have been considering the make-up of purposes and results that constitute conduct—its "what." But conduct has a certain method and spirit also—its "how." Conduct may be looked upon as expressing the attitudes and dispositions of an *individual*, as well as realizing social results and maintaining the social fabric. A consideration of conduct as a mode of individual performance, personal doing, takes us from the social to the psychological side of morals. In the first place, all conduct springs ultimately and radically out of native instincts and impulses. We must know what these instincts and impulses are, and what they are at each particular stage of the child's development, in order to know what to appeal to and what to build upon. Neglect of this principle may give a mechanical imitation of moral conduct, but the imitation will be ethically dead, because it is external and has its centre without, not within, the individual. We must study the child, in other words, to get our indications, our symptoms, our suggestions. The more or less spontaneous acts of the child are not to be thought of as setting moral forms to which the efforts of the educator must conform—this would result simply in spoiling the child; but they are symptoms which require to be interpreted: stimuli which need to be responded to in directed ways; material which, in however transformed a shape, is the only ultimate constituent of future moral conduct and character.

Then, secondly, our ethical principles need to be stated in psychological terms because the child supplies us with the only means or instruments by which to realize moral ideals. The subject-matter of the curriculum, however important, however judiciously selected, is empty of conclusive moral content until it is made over into terms of the individual's own activities, habits, and desires. We must know what history, geography, and mathematics mean in psychological terms, that is, as modes of personal experiencing, before we can get out of them their moral potentialities.

The psychological side of education sums itself up, of course, in a consideration of character. It is a commonplace to say that the development of character is the end of all school work. The difficulty lies in the execution of the idea. And an underlying difficulty in this execution is the lack of a clear conception of what character means. This may seem an extreme statement. If so, the idea may be conveyed by saying that we generally conceive of character simply in terms of results; we have no clear conception of it in psychological terms—that is, as a process, as working or dynamic. We know what character means in terms of the actions which proceed from it, but we have not a definite conception of it on its inner side, as a system of working forces.

(1) Force, efficiency in execution, or overt action, is one necessary constituent of character. In our moral books and lectures we may lay the stress upon good intentions, etc. But we know practically that the kind of character we hope to build up through our education is one that not only has good intentions, but that insists upon carrying them out. Any other character is wishy-washy; it is goody, not good. The individual must have the power to stand up and count for something in the actual conflicts of life. He must have initiative, insistence, persistence, courage, and industry. He must, in a word, have all that goes under the name "*force* of character." Undoubtedly, individuals differ greatly in their native endowment in this respect. None the less, each has a certain primary equipment of impulse, of tendency forward, of

innate urgency to do. The problem of education on this side is that of discovering what this native fund of power is, and then of utilizing it in such a way (affording conditions which both stimulate and control) as to organize it into definite conserved modes of action—habits.

(2) But something more is required than sheer force. Sheer force may be brutal; it may override the interests of others. Even when aiming at right ends it may go at them in such a way as to violate the rights of others. More than this, in sheer force there is no guarantee for the right end. Efficiency may be directed towards mistaken ends and result in positive mischief and destruction. Power, as already suggested, must be directed. It must be organized along social channels; it must be attached to valuable ends.

This involves training on both the intellectual and emotional side. On the intellectual side we must have judgment—what is ordinarily called good sense. The difference between mere knowledge, or information, and judgment is that the former is simply held, not used; judgment is knowledge directed with reference to the accomplishment of ends. Good judgment is a sense of respective or proportionate values. The one who has judgment is the one who has ability to size up a situation. He is the one who can grasp the scene or situation before him, ignoring what is irrelevant, or what for the time being is unimportant, who can seize upon the factors which demand attention, and grade them according to their respective claims. Mere knowledge of what the right is, in the abstract, mere intentions of following the right in general, however praiseworthy in themselves, are never a substitute for this power of trained judgment. Action is always in the concrete. It is definite and individualized. Except, therefore, as it is backed and controlled by a knowledge of the actual concrete factors in the situation in which it occurs, it must be relatively futile and waste.

(3) But the consciousness of ends must be more than merely intellectual. We can imagine a person with most excellent judgment, who yet does not act upon his judgment. There must not only be force to ensure effort in execution against obstacles, but there must also be a delicate personal responsiveness,—there must be an emotional reaction. Indeed, good judgment is impossible without this susceptibility. Unless there

is a prompt and almost instinctive sensitiveness to conditions, to the ends and interests of others, the intellectual side of judgment will not have proper material to work upon. Just as the material of knowledge is supplied through the senses, so the material of ethical knowledge is supplied by emotional responsiveness. It is difficult to put this quality into words, but we all know the difference between the character which is hard and formal, and one which is sympathetic, flexible, and open. In the abstract the former may be as sincerely devoted to moral ideas as is the latter, but as a practical matter we prefer to live with the latter. We count upon it to accomplish more by tact, by instinctive recognition of the claims of others, by skill in adjusting, than the former can accomplish by mere attachment to rules.

Here, then, is the moral standard, by which to test the work of the school upon the side of what it does directly for individuals. (a) Does the school as a system, at present, attach sufficient importance to the spontaneous instincts and impulses? Does it afford sufficient opportunity for these to assert themselves and work out their own results? Can we even say that the school in principle attaches itself, at present, to the active constructive powers rather than to processes of absorption and learning? Does not our talk about self-activity largely render itself meaningless because the self-activity we have in mind is purely "intellectual," out of relation to those impulses which work through hand and eye?

Just in so far as the present school methods fail to meet the test of such questions moral results must be unsatisfactory. We cannot secure the development of positive force of character unless we are willing to pay its price. We cannot smother and repress the child's powers, or gradually abort them (from failure of opportunity for exercise), and then expect a character with initiative and consecutive industry. I am aware of the importance attaching to inhibition, but mere inhibition is valueless. The only restraint, the only holding-in, that is of any worth is that which comes through holding powers concentrated upon a positive end. An end cannot be attained excepting as instincts and impulses are kept from discharging at random and from running off on side tracks. In keeping powers at work upon their relevant ends, there is sufficient opportunity for genuine inhibition. To say that inhibition is higher than power, is like saying that death is more than life, negation more than affirmation, sacrifice more than service.

(b) We must also test our school work by finding whether it affords the conditions necessary for the formation of good judgment. Judgment as the sense of relative values involves ability to select, to discriminate. Acquiring information can never develop the power of judgment. Development of judgment is in spite of, not because of, methods of instruction that emphasize simple learning. The test comes only when the information acquired has to be put to use. Will it do what we expect of it? I have heard an educator of large experience say that in her judgment the greatest defect of instruction to-day, on the intellectual side, is found in the fact that children leave school without a mental perspective. Facts seem to them all of the same importance. There is no foreground or background. There is no instinctive habit of sorting out facts upon a scale of worth and of grading them.

The child cannot get power of judgment excepting as he is continually exercised in forming and testing judgments. He must have an opportunity to select for himself, and to attempt to put his selections into execution, that he may submit them to the final test, that of action. Only thus can he learn to discriminate that which promises success from that which promises failure; only thus can he form the habit of relating his purposes and notions to the conditions that determine their value. Does the school, as a system, afford at present sufficient opportunity for this sort of experimentation? Except so far as the emphasis of the school work is upon intelligent doing, upon active investigation, it does not furnish the conditions necessary for that exercise of judgment which is an integral factor in good character.

(c) I shall be brief with respect to the other point, the need of susceptibility and responsiveness. The informally social side of education, the æsthetic environment and influences, are all-important. In so far as the work is laid out in regular and formulated ways, so far as there are lacking opportunities for casual and free social intercourse between pupils and between the pupils and the teacher, this side of the child's nature is either starved, or else left to find haphazard expression along more or less secret channels. When the school system, under plea of the practical (meaning by the practical the narrowly utilitarian), confines the child to the three R's and the formal studies connected with them, shuts him out from the vital in literature and history, and deprives him of his right to contact with what is best in architecture, music, sculpture, and picture, it is hopeless to expect definite results in the training of sympathetic openness and responsiveness.

* * * *

What we need in education is a genuine faith in the existence of moral principles which are capable of effective application. We believe, so far as the mass of children are concerned, that if we keep at them long enough we can teach reading and writing and figuring. We are practically, even if unconsciously, skeptical as to the possibility of anything like the same assurance in morals. We believe in moral laws and rules, to be sure, but they are in the air. They are something set off by themselves. They are so *very* "moral" that they have no working contact with the average affairs of every-day life. These moral principles need to be brought down to the ground through their statement in social and in psychological terms. We need to see that moral principles are not arbitrary, that they are not "transcendental"; that the term "moral" does not designate a special region or portion of life. We need to translate the moral into the conditions and forces of our community life, and into the impulses and habits of the individual.

All the rest is mint, anise, and cummin. The one thing needful is that we recognize that moral principles are real in the same sense in which other forces are real; that they are inherent in community life, and in the working structure of the individual. If we can secure a genuine faith in this fact, we shall have secured the condition which alone is necessary to get from our educational system all the effectiveness there is in it. The teacher who operates in this faith will find every subject, every method of instruction, every incident of school life pregnant with moral possibility.

MY PEDAGOGIC CREED

What Education Is

I believe that all education proceeds by the participation of the individual in the social consciousness of the race. This process begins unconsciously almost at birth, and is continually shaping the individuals powers, saturating his consciousness, forming his habits, training his ideas, and arousing his feelings and emotions. Through this unconscious education the individual gradually comes to share in the intellectual and moral resources which humanity has succeeded in getting together. He becomes an inheritor of the funded capital of civilization. The most formal and technical education in the world cannot safely depart from this general process. It can only organize it; or differentiate it in some particular direction.

I believe that the only true education comes through the stimulation of the child's powers by the demands of the social situations in which he finds himself. Through these demands he is stimulated to act as a member of a unity, to emerge from his original narrowness of action and feeling, and to conceive of himself from the standpoint of the welfare of the group to which he belongs. Through the responses which others make to his own activities he comes to know what these mean in social terms. The value which they have is reflected back into them. For instance, through the response which is made to the child's instinctive babblings the child comes to know what those babblings mean; they are transformed into articulate language, and thus the child is introduced into the consolidated wealth of ideas and emotions which are now summed up in language.

I believe that this educational process has two sides—one psychological and one sociological; and that neither can be subordinated to the other or neglected without evil results following. Of these two sides, the psychological is the basis. The child's own instincts and powers furnish the material and give the starting-point for all education. Save as the efforts of the educator connect with some activity which the child is carrying on of his own initiative independent of the educator, education becomes reduced to a pressure from without. It may, indeed, give certain external results, but cannot truly be called educative. Without insight into the psychological structure and activities of the individual, the educative process will, therefore, be haphazard and arbitrary. If it chances to coincide with the child's activity it will get a leverage; if it does not, it will result in friction, or disintegration, or arrest of the child nature.

> *The child's own instincts and powers furnish the material and give the starting point for all education.*

I believe that knowledge of social conditions, of the present state of civilization, is necessary in order properly to interpret the child's powers. The child has his own instincts and tendencies, but we do not know what these mean until we can translate them into their social equivalents. We must be able to carry them back into a social past and see them as the inheritance of previous race activities. We must also be able to project them into the future to see what their outcome and end will be. In the illustration just used, it is the ability to see in the child's babblings the promise and potency of a future social intercourse and conversation which enables one to deal in the proper way with that instinct.

I believe that the psychological and social sides are organically related, and that education cannot be regarded as a compromise between the two, or a superimposition of one upon the other. We are told that the psychological definition of education is barren and, formal—that it gives us only the idea of a development of all the mental powers without giving us any idea of the use to which these powers are put. On the other hand, it is urged that the social definition of education, as getting adjusted to civilization, makes of it a forced and external process, and results in subordinating the freedom of the individual to a preconceived social and political status.

I believe each of these objections is true when urged against one side isolated from the other. In order to know what a power really is we must know what its end, use, or function is; and this we cannot know save as we conceive of the individual as active in social relationships. But, on the other hand, the only possible adjustment which we can give to the child under existing conditions, is that which arises through putting him in complete possession of all his powers. With the advent of democracy and modern industrial conditions, it is impossible to foretell definitely just what civilization will be twenty years from now. Hence it is impossible to prepare the child for any precise set of conditions. To prepare him for the future life means to give him command of himself; it means so to train him that he will have the full and really use of all his capacities; that his eye and ear and hand may be tools ready to command, that his judgment may be capable of grasping the conditions under which it has to work, and the executive forces be trained to act economically and efficiently. It is impossible to reach this sort of adjustment save as constant regard is had to the individual's own powers, tastes, and interests—say, that is, as education is continually converted into psychological terms.

In sum, I believe that the individual who is to be educated is a social individual, and that society is an organic union of individuals. If we eliminate the social factor from the child we are left only with an abstraction; if we eliminate the individual factor from society, we are left only with an inert and lifeless mass. Education, therefore, must begin with a psychological insight into the child's capacities, interests, and habits. It must be controlled at every point by reference to these same considerations. These powers, interests, and habits must be continually interpreted—we must know what they mean. They must be translated into terms of their social equivalents—into terms of what they are capable of in the way of social service.

What the School Is

I believe that the school is primarily a social institution. Education being a social process, the school is simply that form of community life in which all those agencies are concentrated that will be most effective in bringing the child to share in the inherited resources of the race, and to use his own powers for social ends.

I believe that education... is a process of living and not a preparation for future living.

I believe that education, therefore, is a process of living and not a preparation for future living.

I believe that the school must represent present life—life as real and vital to the child as that which he carries on in the home, in the neighborhood, or on the playground.

I believe that education which does not occur through forms of life, forms that are worth living for their own sake, is always a poor substitute for the genuine reality, and tends to cramp and to deaden.

I believe that the school, as an institution, should simplify existing social life; should reduce it, as it were, to an embryonic form. Existing life is so complex that the child cannot be brought into contact with it without either confusion or distraction; he is either overwhelmed by the multiplicity of activities which are going on, so that he loses his own power of orderly reaction, or he is so stimulated by these various activities that his powers are prematurely called into play and he becomes either unduly specialized or else disintegrated.

I believe that, as such simplified social life, the school life should grow gradually out of the home life; that it should take up and continue the activities with which the child is already familiar in the home.

I believe that it should exhibit these activities to the child, and reproduce them in such ways that the child will gradually learn the meaning of them, and be capable of playing his own part in relation to them.

I believe that this is a psychological necessity, because it is the only way of securing continuity in the child's growth, the only way of giving a background of past experience to the new ideas given in school.

I believe it is also a social necessity because the home is the form of social life in which the child has been nurtured and in connection with which he has had his moral training. It is the business of the school to deepen and extend his sense of the values bound up in his home life.

I believe that much of present education fails because it neglects this fundamental principle of the school as a form of community life. It conceives the school as a place where certain information is to be given, where certain lessons are to be learned, or where certain habits are to be formed. The value of these is conceived as lying largely in the remote future; the child must do these things for the sake of something else he is to do; they are mere preparations. As a result they do not become a part of the life experience of the child and so are not truly educative.

I believe that the moral education centers upon this conception of the school as a mode of social life, that the best and deepest moral training is precisely that which one gets through having to enter into proper relations with others in a unity of work and thought. The present educational systems, so far as they destroy or neglect this unity, render it difficult or impossible to get any genuine, regular moral training.

I believe that the child should be stimulated and controlled in his work through the life of the community.

I believe that under existing conditions far too much of the stimulus and control proceeds from the teacher, because of neglect of the idea of the school as a form of social life.

I believe that the teacher's place and work in the school is to be interpreted from this same basis. The teacher is not in the school to impose certain ideas or to form certain habits in the child, but is there as a member of the community to select the influences which shall affect the child and to assist him in properly responding to these influences.

I believe that the discipline of the school should proceed from the life of the school as a whole and not directly from the teacher.

I believe that the teacher's business is simply to determine, on the basis of larger experience and riper wisdom, how the discipline of life shall come to the child.

I believe that all questions of the grading of the child and his promotion should be determined by reference to the same standard. Examinations are of use only so far as they test the child's fitness for social life and reveal the place in which he can be of the most service and where he can receive the most help.

The Subject-Matter
Of Education

I believe that the social life of the child is the basis of concentration, or correlation, in all his training or growth. The social life gives the unconscious unity and the background of all his efforts and of all his attainments.

I believe that the subject-matter of the school curriculum should mark a gradual differentiation out of the primitive unconscious unity of social life.

I believe that we violate the child's nature and render difficult the best ethical results by introducing the child too abruptly to a number of special studies, of reading, writing, geography, etc., out of relation to this social life.

I believe, therefore, that the true center of correlation on the school subjects is not science, nor literature, nor history, nor geography, but the child's own social activities.

I believe that education cannot be unified in the study of science, or so-called nature study, because apart from human activity, nature itself is not a unity; nature in itself is a number of diverse objects in space and time, and to attempt to make it the center of work by itself is to introduce a principle of radiation rather than one of concentration.

I believe that literature is the reflex expression and interpretation of social experience; that hence it must follow upon and not precede such experience. It, therefore, cannot be made the basis, although it may be made the summary of unification.

I believe once more that history is of educative value in so far as it presents phases of social life and growth. It must be controlled by reference to social life. When taken simply as history it is thrown into the distant past and becomes dead and inert. Taken as the record of man's social life and progress it becomes full of meaning. I believe, however, that it cannot be so taken excepting as the child is also introduced directly into social life.

I believe accordingly that the primary basis of education is in the child's powers at work along the same general constructive lines as those which have brought civilization into being.

I believe that the only way to make the child conscious of his social heritage is to enable him to perform those fundamental types of activity which make civilization what it is.

I believe, therefore, in the so-called expressive or constructive activities as the center of correlation.

I believe that this gives the standard for the place of cooking, sewing, manual training, etc., in the school.

I believe that they are not special studies which are to be introduced over and above a lot of others in the way of relaxation or relief, or as additional accomplishments. I believe rather that they represent, as types, fundamental forms of social activity; and that it is possible and desirable that the child's introduction into the more formal subjects of the curriculum be through the medium of these activities.

I believe that the study of science is educational in so far as it brings out the materials and processes which make social life what it is.

I believe that one of the greatest difficulties in the present teaching of science is that the material is presented in purely objective form, or is treated as a new peculiar kind of experience which the child can add to that which he has already had. In reality, science is of value because it gives the ability to interpret and control the experience already had. It should be introduced, not as so much new subject-matter, but as showing the factors already involved in previous experience and as furnishing tools by which that experience can be more easily and effectively regulated.

I believe that at present we lose much of the value of literature and language studies because of our elimination of the social element. Language is almost always treated in the books of pedagogy simply as the expression of thought. It is true that language is a logical instrument, but it is fundamentally and primarily a social instrument. Language is the device for communication; it is the tool through which one individual comes to share the ideas and feelings of others. When treated simply as a way of getting individual information, or as a means of showing off what one has learned, it loses its social motive and end.

I believe that there is, therefore, no succession of studies in the ideal school curriculum. If education is life, all life has, from the outset, a scientific aspect; an aspect of art and culture and an aspect of communication. It cannot, therefore, be true that the proper studies for one grade are mere reading and writing, and that at a later grade, reading, or literature, or science, may be introduced. The progress is not in the succession of studies, but in the development of new attitudes towards, and new interests in, experience.

I believe, finally, that education must be conceived as a continuing reconstruction of experience; that the process and the goal of education are one and the same thing.

I believe that to set up any end outside of education, as furnishing its goal and standard, is to deprive the educational process of much of its meaning, and tends to make us rely upon false and external stimuli in dealing with the child.

The Nature of Method

I believe that the question of method is ultimately reducible to the question of the order of development of the child's powers and interests. The law for presenting and treating material is the law implicit within the child's own nature. Because this is so I believe the following statements are of supreme importance as determining the spirit in which education is carried on:

1. I believe that the active side precedes the passive in the development of the child-nature; that expression comes before conscious impression; that the muscular development precedes the sensory; that movements come before conscious sensations; I believe that consciousness is essentially motor or impulsive; that conscious states tend to project themselves in action.

   I believe that the neglect of this principle is the cause of a large part of the waste of time and strength in school work. The child is thrown into a passive, receptive, or absorbing attitude. The conditions are such that he is not permitted to follow the law of his nature; the result is friction and waste.

I believe that ideas (intellectual and rational processes) also result from action and devolve for the sake of the better control of action. What we term reason is primarily the law of orderly or effective action. To attempt to develop the reasoning powers, the powers of judgment, without reference to the selection and arrangement of means in action, is the fundamental fallacy in our present methods of dealing with this matter. As a result we present the child with arbitrary symbols. Symbols are a necessity in mental development, but they have their place as tools for economizing effort; presented by themselves they are a mass of meaningless and arbitrary ideas imposed from without.

2. I believe that the image is the great instrument of instruction. What a child gets out of any subject presented to him is simply the images which he himself forms with regard to it.

I believe that if nine-tenths of the energy at present directed towards making the child learn certain things were spent in seeing to it that the child was forming proper images, the work of instruction would be indefinitely facilitated.

I believe that much of the time and attention now given to the preparation and presentation of lessons might be more wisely and profitably expended in training the child's power of imagery and in seeing to it that he was continually forming definite, vivid, and growing images of the various subjects with which he comes in contact in his experience.

3. I believe that interests are the signs and symptoms of growiug power. I believe that they represent dawning capacities. Accordingly the constant and careful observation of interests is of the utmost importance for the educator.

I believe that these interests are to be observed as showing the state of development which the child has reached.

I believe that they prophesy the stage upon which he is about to enter.

I believe that only through the continual and sympathetic observation of childhood's interests can the adult enter into the child's life and see what it is ready for, and upon what material it could work most readily and fruitfully.

I believe that these interests are neither to be humored nor repressed. To repress interest is to substitute the adult for the child, and so to weaken intellectual curiosity and alertness, to suppress initiative, and to deaden interest. To humor the interests is to substitute the transient for the permanent. The interest is always the sign of some power below; the important thing is to discover this power. To humor the interest is to fail to penetrate below the surface, and its sure result is to substitute caprice and whim for genuine interest.

> *To repress interest is to substitute the adult for the child, and so to weaken intellectual curiosity and alertness, to suppress initiative, and to deaden interest.*

4. I believe that the emotions are the reflex of actions.

I believe that to endeavor to stimulate or arouse the emotions apart from their corresponding activities is to introduce an unhealthy and morbid state of mind.

I believe that if we can only secure right habits of action and thought, with reference to the good, the true, and the beautiful, the emotions will for the most part take care of themselves.

I believe that next to deadness and dullness, formalism and routine, our education is threatened with no greater evil than sentimentalism.

I believe that this sentimentalism is the necessary result of the attempt to divorce feeling from action.

The School and Social Progress

I believe that education is the fundamental method of social progress and reform.

I believe that all reforms which rest simply upon the enactment of law, or the threatening of certain penalties, or upon changes in mechanical or outward arrangements, are transitory and futile.

I believe that education is a regulation of the process of coming to share in the social consciousness; and that the adjustment of individual activity on the basis of this social consciousness is the only sure method of social reconstruction.

> *I believe that education is the fundamental method of social progress and reform.*

I believe that this conception has due regard for both the individualistic and socialistic ideals. It is duly individual because it recognizes the formation of a certain character as the only genuine basis of right living. It is socialistic because it recognizes that this right character is not to be formed by merely individual precept, example, or exhortation, but rather by the influence of

48

a certain form of institutional or community life upon the individual, and that the social organism through the school, as its organ, may determine ethical results.

I believe that in the ideal school we have the reconciliation of the individualistic and the institutional ideals.

I believe that the community's duty to education is, therefore, its paramount moral duty. By law and punishment, by social agitation and discussion, society can regulate and form itself in a more or less haphazard and chance way. But through education society can formulate its own purposes, can organize its own means and resources, and thus shape itself with definiteness and economy in the direction in which it wishes to move.

> *I believe that all reforms which rest simply upon the enactment of law, or the threatening of certain penalties, or upon changes in mechanical or outward arrangements, are transitory and futile.*

I believe that when society once recognizes the possibilities in this direction, and the obligations which these possibilities impose, it is impossible to conceive of the resources of time, attention, and money which will be put at the disposal of the educator.

I believe it is the business of every one interested in education to insist upon the school as the primary and most effective interest of social progress and reform in order that society may be awakened to realize what the school stands for, and aroused to the necessity of endowing the educator with sufficient equipment properly to perform his task.

I believe that education thus conceived marks the most perfect and intimate union of science and art conceivable in human experience.

I believe that the art of thus giving shape to human powers and adapting them to social service is the supreme art; one calling into its service the best of artists; that no insight, sympathy, tact, executive power is too great for such service.

I believe that with the growth of psychological service, giving added insight into individual structure and laws of growth; and with growth of social science, adding to our knowledge of the right organization of individuals, all scientific resources can be utilized for the purposes of education.

I believe that when science and art thus join hands the most commanding motive for human action will be reached; the most genuine springs of human conduct aroused, and the best service that human nature is capable of guaranteed.

I believe, finally, that the teacher is engaged, not simply in the training of individuals, but in the formation of the proper social life.

I believe that every teacher should realize the dignity of his calling; that he is a social servant set apart for the maintenance of proper social order and the securing of the right social growth.

I believe that in this way the teacher always is the prophet of the true God and the usherer in of the true kingdom of God.